Police Officer

Jeff Barger

Rourke
Educational Media
rourkeeducationalmedia.com

A Division of
Carson Dellosa
Education.

Before Reading: *Building Background Knowledge and Vocabulary*

Building background knowledge can help children process new information and build upon what they already know. Before reading a book, it is important to tap into what children already know about the topic. This will help them develop their vocabulary and increase their reading comprehension.

Questions and Activities to Build Background Knowledge:

1. Look at the front cover of the book and read the title. What do you think this book will be about?
2. What do you already know about this topic?
3. Take a book walk and skim the pages. Look at the table of contents, photographs, captions, and bold words. Did these text features give you any information or predictions about what you will read in this book?

Vocabulary: *Vocabulary Is Key to Reading Comprehension*

Use the following directions to prompt a conversation about each word.

- Read the vocabulary words.
- What comes to mind when you see each word?
- What do you think each word means?

> ## Vocabulary Words:
> - *authority*
> - *crosswalk*
> - *laws*
> - *traffic*

During Reading: *Reading for Meaning and Understanding*

To achieve deep comprehension of a book, children are encouraged to use close reading strategies. During reading, it is important to have children stop and make connections. These connections result in deeper analysis and understanding of a book.

 Close Reading a Text

During reading, have children stop and talk about the following:

- Any confusing parts
- Any unknown words
- Text to text, text to self, text to world connections
- The main idea in each chapter or heading

Encourage children to use context clues to determine the meaning of any unknown words. These strategies will help children learn to analyze the text more thoroughly as they read.

When you are finished reading this book, turn to the next-to-last page for an **After Reading Activity**.

Table of Contents

Community Helpers

Community helpers are all around us.
They make our lives better.

People who live or work in the same area are part of a community.

Police officers protect us.

Laws

Laws are rules for citizens.

Police officers make sure we follow laws.

Citizens are the members of a community.

Laws keep us safe.

Where can we cross a street? A law tells us where.

The law says you must use a **crosswalk**.

Different Jobs

Police officers do many jobs.

They teach us about laws.

Police officers go to schools to teach students.

Police officers direct **traffic**.

They tell drivers where to go.

Officers use hand signals to direct traffic.

Some officers drive cars. Some ride motorcycles.

Police officers use lights and sirens to alert people.

Police officers wear a uniform.

There is a badge on the uniform.

A badge is a symbol of authority.

Police officers solve problems.

They keep us from harm each day.

Activity

A New Community

Supplies
- markers
- paper
- pencil

Directions
Imagine you are in charge of starting a new community. Think about laws that are important for keeping community members safe. Write or draw five laws that you will need to have before you build your community.

Photo Glossary

 **authority** (uh-THOR-i-tee): The power to do something officially or to tell other people what to do.

 **crosswalk** (KRAWS-wawk): A place where pedestrians can safely cross a street, often marked with painted lines.

 **laws** (laws): Rules established and enforced by a government.

 **traffic** (TRAF-ik): All the moving vehicles on a particular road at a particular time.

Index

After Reading Activity

Laws are rules for a community. What rules do you have in your classroom? What is a rule that you would add? Think about your school and list three rules that you think would be good for your school.

About the Author

Jeff Barger is an author, blogger, and literacy specialist. He lives in North Carolina. Jeff is grateful for the police officers that protect communities everyhwere.

www.rourkeeducationalmedia.com

Edited by: Kim Thompson
Cover and interior design by: Kathy Walsh

Photo Credits: Cover, title page, p.7, 20, 22: ©kali9; p.5: ©Rawpixel.com; p.9, 22: ©RyanJLane; p.11, 22: ©monkeybusinessimages; p.13: ©Steve Debenport; p.15, 22: ©kaarsten; p.17: ©andrearoad; p.19: ©Sean Locke Photography

Library of Congress PCN Data

Police Officer / Jeff Barger
(Community Helpers)
ISBN 978-1-73161-415-5 (hard cover)(alk. paper)
ISBN 978-1-73161-210-6 (soft cover)
ISBN 978-1-73161-520-6 (e-Book)
ISBN 978-1-73161-625-8 (ePub)
Library of Congress Control Number: 2019932036

Rourke Educational Media
Printed in the United States of America,
North Mankato, Minnesota